WALKING CORNWALL

WITH DONALD VAGE
BOOK THREE

FOURTEEN
CORNISH COUNTRYSIDE
& COASTAL WALKS
WITH MAPS & PHOTOGRAPHS

CORNWALL BOOKS

First published in 1992 by Cornwall Books
Copyright © Donald Vage, 1992

British Library Cataloguing in Publication Data

CIP Data for this book is available from the British Library

ISBN 1 871060 15X

CORNWALL BOOKS

An imprint of Westcountry Books
Chinon Court
Lower Moor Way
Tiverton
Devon EX16 6SS

Tel: 0884 243242
Fax: 0884 243325

*Cover illustration: Author and his wife at Garrow Farm
near St Breward (see Walk 9).*

Designed for Cornwall Books by
TOPICS Visual Information
397 Topsham Road
Exeter EX2 6HD
Telephone 0392 876800

Typeset in Great Britain by ICON, Exeter

Printed and bound in Great Britain by BPCC Wheatons Ltd., Exeter.

BOOK THREE
CONTENTS

Location of the fourteen walks.

FOREWORD

To be able to share with the reader the pleasures of walking is something worthwhile to me. I hope that readers will also discover a variety of interesting things on these walks that I have not mentioned in these descriptions. This third book is one of startling contrasts – of dramatic coast and seas; lonely moors and soft green valleys; rocky tors and flat water meadows – and always a little away from the 'honey pot' tourist areas. The different seasons give such variety to the walks; I hope the walks can be repeated without even a hint of boredom.

As in my previous books, I suggest that the following things are important for your enjoyment and safety: good boots, maps and compass, waterproof clothing, emergency rations and clothes, and a respect for the Country Code and other people's property. The maps included in this book are intended only as rough guides – I would strongly recommend using the Ordnance Survey 1:50 000 maps (or the even more detailed 1:25 000 series); you will then be able to ensure that you are keeping to public rights of way.

In a world of increasing pace and noise and pollution, my thoughts follow those of Shelley, who wrote:
'I love all waste and solitary places
Where we taste
The pleasures of believing all we see
Is boundless, as we wish our souls to be.'
These walks can be likened to just a few of the golden eggs laid by Cornwall's 'Golden Goose'. It is up to us to see that nothing spoils them for our grandchildren and their grandchildren.

WALK ONE

A coastal, creekside and country walk.
PORTHALLOW TO GILLAN
OS Map (1:50,000) 204 or OS Map (1:25,000) SW 72/82
Length: approximately five miles.

For the first walk – one of our best-loved – we head for the east side of the Lizard peninsula. It starts at the little fishing village of Porthallow (known locally as 'Praala'), a short distance north of St Keverne.

It is not the easiest village to find, but that all adds to the enjoyment. Generally speaking, head for Helston, then St Keverne, and a mile or so before reaching the spire of the church you will see a sign to Porthallow.

Behind the shingle beach, in a cluster of cottages, is the friendly Five Pilchards inn where you can see photographs of wrecks in the area. The dreaded Manacles Rocks are only a couple of miles to the south.

This village has many memories for my wife and I as it was here that we came in my late brother's boat from Malpas, firstly Dawn and then Joyance, over twenty years ago, and many a good swim and happy day we have had here.

To the north of the beach, a flight of

The car park and beach at Porthallow.

View from the beach at Porthallow with Nare Head in the middle distance and St Anthony Lighthouse and Zone Point in the far distance.

steps leads up to the coastal footpath which rises and dips towards Nare Point to the continual background song of the skylark. In spring the footpath is bordered by masses of bluebells and red campions among the uncurling bracken. In summer you walk between fields of standing wheat and barley with the occasional poppy on the verge of the footpath, and on the other side gorse, honeysuckle and foxgloves, right to the cliff edge.

On the high ground, just before you drop down to Nare Point, pause to enjoy the view northwards of hundreds of sailing craft around the mouth of the Helford River. To the north-east is St Mawes with the white clay-waste mountains of St Austell beyond, Zone Point with St Anthony lighthouse, Nare Head and even the Dodman in the misty distance.

After walking round the low headland of Nare Point, head west along the foot

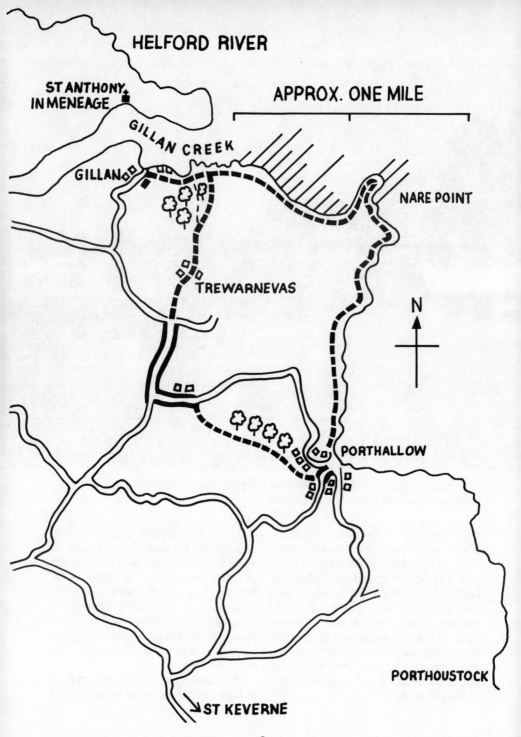

HELFORD RIVER

ST ANTHONY
IN MENEAGE

GILLAN CREEK

GILLAN

APPROX. ONE MILE

NARE POINT

TREWARNEVAS

N

PORTHALLOW

PORTHOUSTOCK

ST KEVERNE

8

Looking across to Gillan Harbour from Dennis Head.

of a steep field, over a stile and along-side the estuary of the Helford River towards Gillan Harbour. At low tide the jagged rocks of Men-aver Point are a reminder of how dangerous this coast can be to the unwary.

As the footpath leads over higher land above the entrance to Gillan Creek, you can look across to the fifteenth-century church of St Anthony and Dennis Head with its ruined fort built by Henry VIII to protect the flank of Pendennis Castle.

The path now descends some steps under trees to a headland and round to Flushing, a tiny hamlet of houses backed by oak and pine trees. Around a second headland and behind some houses, the path descends to Gillan Harbour and a winding road that leads back to Porthallow.

But to complete our walk, we usually walk back to Flushing, round the rocky headland and up the steps. At the top, just below a house, instead of retracing your steps along the coast, keep straight on beside a garden and follow the bridle-path along the valleyside until you reach Trewarnevas farm. Passing through the farmyard, you soon reach a minor road where you head south across rolling farmland.

View across Gillan Creek towards St Anthony in Meneage.

Take the first turning on your left and walk east to Treglossick farm. On the right, opposite the last of the farm buildings, stands a tree, beyond which some steps in a wall by a gate lead to a footpath across a field. This is very easy to miss, the last time I walked this way there was no footpath sign.
You now follow a most beautiful valley beside a stream and over two little bridges right back to Porthallow. This is a most peaceful stretch of walking country and at certain times of the day, the bird-song is almost deafening.

Back in Porthallow, right opposite the post office, we usually sit and enjoy a jam and cream tea under bright umbrellas in the garden of a house with the New Zealand name of 'Taranaki'. If you are in need of liquid refreshment, you might want to head back to the Five Pilchards, with its nautical artefacts and maritime pictures.

On our last walk along this stretch of coast we were very conscious that all the paths had been cleared and tidied and we gave our thanks to both the local council and the National Trust.

WALK TWO

From harbour to headland, past one of Cornwall's most feared sandbanks.
PADSTOW TO STEPPER POINT AND GUNVER HEAD
OS Map (1:50,000) 200 or OS Map (1:25,000) SW 87/97
Length: approximately six miles.

We began this walk at the same point that we began our epic Saints' Way walk across Cornwall, from Padstow to Fowey. (Those of you who read Book Two in this series may have enjoyed it for yourself). But this time we are heading north to the mouth of the River Camel and the sea.

Padstow inner harbour at high tide showing the sixteenth-century building associated with Sir Walter Raleigh.

You can leave your car right on the quayside, near the sixteenth-century Courthouse associated with Sir Walter Raleigh. With its delightful 12-paned windows and uneven roof, it is one of Padstow's many treasures.

After rounding the harbour, we set off seaward, up the hill to the war memorial on its little hillock. From this vantage point you can look over the River Camel to Rock and the parish of St Enodoc whose church, with its little crooked spire, lies just behind the rounded mass of Brea Hill.

Full tide at Padstow with part of the fishing fleet.

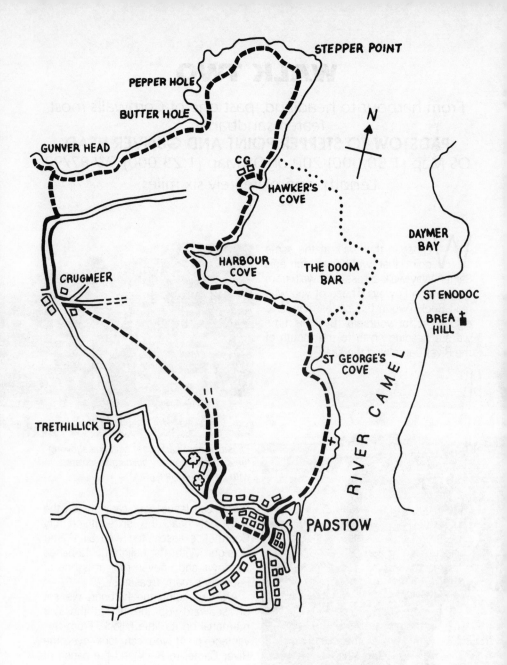

STEPPER POINT

PEPPER HOLE

BUTTER HOLE

GUNVER HEAD

CG

HAWKER'S COVE

N

DAYMER BAY

HARBOUR COVE

THE DOOM BAR

CRUGMEER

ST ENODOC

BREA HILL

ST GEORGE'S COVE

TRETHILLICK

RIVER CAMEL

PADSTOW

APPROX. ONE MILE

12

Low tide at Padstow looking towards the village of Rock and Porthilly Cove.

The footpath now leads down to St George's Cove, with its mysterious little holy well, and around the contours of the river bank to Harbour Cove. If the tide is out, you may wish to take a short cut across the sand, but you will have to jump across the stream which bisects the cove. By following the marked route to the head of the cove, you cross two wooden bridges over the stream and keep your feet dry.

The path now climbs to the old lifeboat house from where you can gaze with awe at the dreaded Doom Bar. At low tide this sandbank is exposed, showing the dangers to the approach of Padstow harbour for the unwary. But as the tide rises, surf pounds where, in a few hours, there will be no sign of the hazard. In the past 150 years nearly 300 ships have been stranded or wrecked on this shallow sandbank and half that number of lives have been lost.

The footpath now passes between coastguard houses and climbs steeply up to Stepper Point where a large stack, built as a daymark, serves its purpose well. From here the views are magnificent – across the estuary of the Camel to Polzeath and Pentire Point, with Newland Rock out to sea. As you look back upriver to Brea Hill you can now see the tiny spire of St Enodoc church surrounded by a rectangle of tamarisk trees.

Looking across the estuary of the Camel from Stepper Point towards Polzeath

By following the coastal footpath round the high headland you will find what has become our favourite picnic spot in a small deserted quarry overlooking Pepper Hole and across to Trevose Head, with Gulland Rock offshore. In summer this whole area is covered with a massive carpet of pinks and I always have the feeling that it is a shame to tread on them. Looking down you can see the precarious nesting places of thousands of gulls and a little beach, quite inaccessible to anyone but a mountaineer or a seaman.

To the south is the even larger chasm of Butter Hole, a massive amphitheatre which magnifies the sound of the waves pounding on the rocks below. From near here you can look back across falling ground to the south-east to the Camel Estuary and Rock on the other side. We now follow the well-marked path to Gunver Head from where you can look across the headland of Trevose down the dramatic north coast of Cornwall – a wonderful sight in stormy weather, with sea spray rising and blowing inland.

Butter Hole from the path between Stepper Point towards Gunver Head.

By backtracking a few yards along the path you will see a signpost directing you inland, alongside a stone hedge to a minor metalled road leading to Crugmeer. If conditions are wet underfoot, you may wish to follow this road, turning left at Trethillick, and so back to Padstow skirting the western side of the Prideaux estate.

But if conditions allow, turn left at Crugmeer for a few yards along a farm lane to a stile on the right. You can now follow a straight-as-a-die path across field after field and stile after stile until you reach the lane which runs east of the estate.

Prideaux Place is always a joy to see and is open to the public on certain days during the summer months. It is a quite unspoilt sixteenth-century manor house – occupied by the same family for its entire history – and the estate includes one of Cornwall's few deer parks.

Before descending to the harbour, you may also wish to visit the nearby Tropical Bird and Butterfly Gardens, or the church dedicated to St Petroc. Slate stone from nearby Harlyn Bay was used for its construction and one bench-end depicts a fox preaching to geese, possibly before eating them.

From the church you wend your way back along the narrow streets of the old town to the harbourside. We usually complete our day with a meal of splits, jam and cream, but if you wish to end the walk in style, you could always call in for an evening meal at one of Britain's finest restaurants, the Seafood Restaurant, by the harbour car-park.

WALK THREE

From peaceful creekside woodland to high granite headlands.
A WALK THROUGH ANTHONY-IN-ROSELAND
OS Map (1:50,000) 204 or OS Map (1:25,000) SW83
Length: approximately three and a half or six miles.

Another title for this walk could have been 'From Froe to Froe' since the walk starts and finishes at the small hamlet of that name on the Roseland peninsula.

To approach the start of the walk, drive south along the road from Porthscatho and Gerrans towards St Anthony. You will reach the little inlet from the Percuil River at Froe, and there is a small National Trust car-park on the right, just opposite the path to Towan Beach.

After parking your car, walk back down the hill a little and you will see a footpath sign on the left which leads you across a wooden bridge. A delightful path follows the border of Porth Creek along the base of fields, then through woods and masses of wild flowers.

The footpaths, stiles and steps throughout this walk (and, indeed, on many of the walks in this book) are well maintained by the National Trust and there seems to be a seat every hun-

Looking down on Froe at the start of our walk.

Place Manor glimpsed from the path, with the spire of the church showing above the roof of the house.

dred yards or so on which to rest and enjoy the changing scenery. We also noticed that a lot of tree planting along the riverside ensures that future generations will be able to enjoy the beauty of these riverside woods of oak, beech and pine.

Turning the corner, where Porth Creek joins the Percuil River that bisects the peninsula, we head south, with the town of St Mawes across the water. Just after leaving Drawlers Plantation you will see a path on the left going to Bohortha.

If you wish to enjoy a shorter walk, this footpath leads across two steep fields into a lane which passes through Bohortha and across the road to pick up the coastal footpath round Porthmellin Head and Killigerran Head and so back to the car.

However, to continue the longer walk, take the right-hand path which emerges in front of Place Manor on a little quay. We rested a while here watching oysters being collected on the beach at low tide.

Remembering that Place Manor is a private residence, we skirted it by following the road a short way. Shortly after passing the Place Shellfish Purification Plant, there is a stile on the right and a track through the churchyard to the 'built-in' church. With its little spire and tower, it is dedicated to St Anthony and was built on the site of a

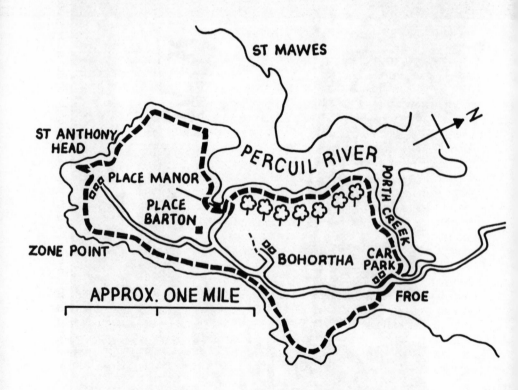

The view of St Anthony Head towards St Mawes and Trefusis Point beyond Carrick Roads.

former ancient monastery. Inside the candle-lit interior of the church we were struck by the memorials to the Spry family (they all seemed to finish up as admirals), the most famous being Sir Richard of the eighteenth century.

Opposite the Norman door of the church a sign bearing the familiar acorn symbol points the way to the footpath which winds under trees round the edge of Cellars Beach. Half-way round this beach a track takes you up and diagonally across a field to a stile in the hedge.

We knew what to expect, but if you are new to this walk, you will be staggered by the view from the top. Suddenly you are gazing over Carrick Roads to Black Rock, Trefusis Point, Pendennis Head and Falmouth docks, and, away in the distance, the Manacles with St Keverne inland.

With this view continually on your right, follow the high coast path southwest, then south, past tall fir trees and above the idyllic little beach at Great Molunan, which rivals any in the West Country. This little stretch of water is a favourite anchorage for family boats, especially when an easterly wind makes the sea 'lumpy' beyond the headland.

After crossing a bridge over a narrow, miniature dam wall, do not climb the steep steps up the hillside, but follow the track behind a sheltering wind-sculpted hedge of blackthorn, to St Anthony lighthouse.

A path climbs to the top of St Anthony Head which still has the remnants of coastal artillery used in wartime right back to Napoleonic times. Some of these buildings have been converted into holiday homes by the

The path near St Anthony Head with St Mawes in the distance.

Picnic beside the path overlooking Porthbeor Beach between Zone Point and Porthmellin Head.

National Trust, which has owned the land since 1959.

Follow the coastal path to Zone Point, where we always stop to study the horizontal table describing various viewpoints. It overlooks all the little fishing boats congregated around an area about a mile out to sea known locally as the 'old walls'.

The footpath now leads north-east along the cliff top to our family's favourite beach, Porthbeor, with its tricky, steep winding path down the cliff side.

We have now reached the point where the shorter walk would have joined the coastal footpath, and if you make your way round the two headlands to Towan Beach, it is only a short walk back to your car.

Perhaps the best point about this walk is that you can walk all day through some of the best scenery in Cornwall, and not see a single car!

WALK FOUR

A walk through Basset country, from high cliff top to deep sheltered woodland.
BASSET COVE TO TEHIDY COUNTRY PARK
OS Map (1:50,000) 203 or OS Map (1:25,000) SW 64
Length: approximately three or six miles.

View from the North Cliffs footpath looking towards Deadman's Cove, Hell's Mouth and Navax Point.

Perhaps a criticism of some of my suggested walks is that they tend to be for a day out rather than half a day, and that most people do not want to tackle more than five miles or so. With this in mind, let us start this walk at Portreath on the north coast.

The harbour was built around 1760 for the export of copper ore and the import of coal from South Wales, for use in the mines. There was once a tramroad between here and Poldice and a connection with the Hayle Railway built in the 1830s; the steep incline up the western side of the valley is still a feature of the landscape. The white 'pepperpot' on the hillside above the narrow entrance to the harbour is a guide to mariners. It is quite difficult to visualise that in the period 1830 to 1848, the whole area had a population of about 30 000.

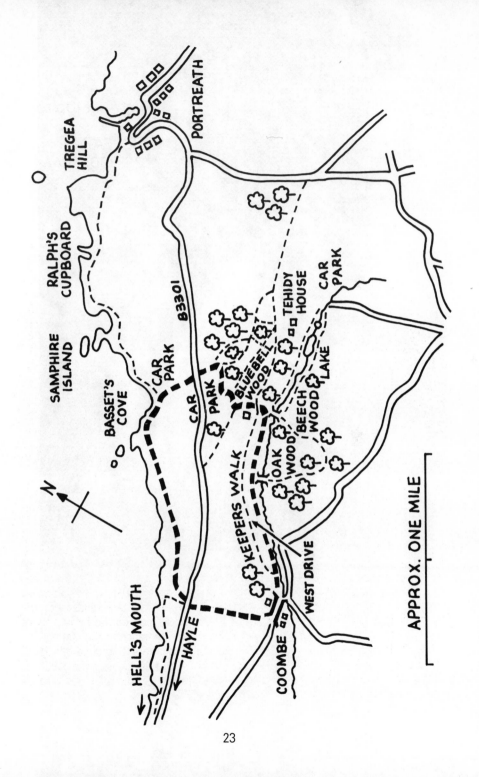

PORTREATH

TREGEA HILL

RALPH'S CUPBOARD

SAMPHIRE ISLAND

BASSET'S COVE

B3301

CAR PARK

CAR PARK

TEHIDY HOUSE

CAR PARK

BLUEBELL WOOD

KEEPERS WALK

BEECH WOOD LAKE

OAK WOOD

HELL'S MOUTH

HAYLE

COOMBE

WEST DRIVE

N

APPROX. ONE MILE

Wintertime walking beside the North Cliffs.

The path near Basset's Cove, with Samphire Island off the path to Portreath.

I have a vivid memory of landing on the RAF airfield to the east of the village in wartime, skimming over the cliff top in a two-engined aircraft and finding the runway 'not overlong'!

We usually buy two excellent, newly made pasties from the bakery in Portreath and, using the 'haybox' principle, we wrap them in the West Briton and car rugs and tuck them into the boot of the car for later consumption.

We now leave Portreath westwards by car on the B3301 for two miles and take the first turning on the right down the unsignposted, unmetalled road to a National Trust car-park at Basset's Cove. An alternative would be to take the cliff path all the way from Portreath, behind Tregea Hill and past Ralph's Cupboard – a collapsed cave. Ralph was presumably a local smuggler, but a Cornish legend attributes the name to a giant called Wrath who would wade out to passing ships and eat the sailors! If you take this route, your return will be along the same path from Basset's Cove, and the walk would be approximately six miles long.

A little further along this alternative route to Basset's Cove we pass Samphire Island, on which once grew a much desired, fleshy-leaved herb. The locals used to clamber and climb onto the island and collect the herb when the seas were less wild than usual.

From the car-park at Basset's Cove our walk leads us south-west along the coast path towards Hell's Mouth, Godrevy Island and the distant sight of Zennor Head. In 1649 Godrevy Island was the scene of a wreck of a ship carrying Charles I's possessions after his execution. Only a man, a boy and a dog survived.

By identifying St Agnes Head with its Coast Guard station you can see offshore Bawden Rocks. I knew them as the Cow and Calf when I used to swim between them as a teenager. Beyond lies Penhale Point with its Gull Rock, the Kelseys with the Chick Rock, and in the far distance is Trevose with a splash of yellow suggesting Constantine beach next to Treyarnon.

Shortly after setting off from Basset's Cove you may notice a low ridge or embankment on the very edge of the cliff – all that remains of an ancient cliff castle. The cliff edge is very precipitous in places, so take care. And if you have a dog with you, keep it on a lead.

When we last walked here in early spring it was bittery cold with frequent hail and sleet showers and a wonderful 'Turner' sky – but we were both suitably clothed.

After a mile of cliff top walking along Reskajeage Downs we turn inland to cross the B3301 to a public footpath notice. We now walk downhill alongside three fields in a direction just east of south until we reach the village of Coombe with the Red River running through it on its way to the sea at Gwithian. Turning left and passing some much-loved gardens we descend and pass to the left of a white house, following a public footpath notice and

The distant coastal path alongside Reskajeage Downs.

26

Bluebell time in Tehidy Woods before the trees are fully in leaf.

some granite pillars – the western entrance to Tehidy Country Park.

There is a fixed all-weather map on the side of the path giving us details of this 250-acre woodland delight with its nine miles of footpaths, camp sites and nature trails. Once part of the land-scaped parkland of Tehidy mansion – home of the Basset family – it was purchased by Cornwall County Council in 1983 and has been carefully restored, with many new landscape features created to transform it into a country park.

It is easy to criticize local government, but let us sometimes give credit to those who had the imagination to buy this land and improve the facilities for Cornish people – in particular its youth. What a site for orienteering!

After 500 yards or so we chose to leave the West Drive and walk steeply uphill to our left to follow the Keeper's Walk through the woods. Our little dog Tessa was overjoyed and was doing a four-times-factor to our mileage, following smells beloved of dachshunds! This path kept reminding me of the Hunter's Path alongside the River Teign on Dartmoor to Fingle Bridge.

We climbed to the Bluebell Wood, which is at its best in April or May of any year, and had a distant view of the Basset Memorial on the summit of Carn Brea. It was erected by subscription in 1836 to Francis Basset who did so much for Cornish mining. We also caught glimpses of the Tehidy mansion, home of the family until 1921, and until recently a hospital.

Using the colour coding at junctions of paths, we made our way up through the woods, past a delightful picnic and barbecue area, to the North Cliffs entrance to the park. We passed perilously close to a swarm of bees hanging from the overhanging branch of a tree!

Almost directly across the B3301 is the rough track to the Basset's Cove car-park. Our pasties were still hot when we reached the car. The warm clothing which we had discarded in the sheltered woods was necessary again in the bitter winds.

For those who want a slightly longer walk and wish to explore more of Tehidy Country Park, a series of routes is suggested on the maps at any of the entrances. Instead of leaving the West Drive, you could continue along it for a short distance before descending to your right and crossing a wooden bridge leading to a walk through Oak Wood.

Alternatively, you could continue along West Drive to Otter Bridge and follow the path to the Cascades and the large lake just below Tehidy mansion. Here there are some delightful bridges, footpaths and small wildfowl lakes, and the whole park is well worth exploring as another countryside walk in itself.

WALK FIVE

A popular walk, via two ferries, through woodland and alongside river and creek.

THE HALL WALK - FROM FOWEY TO POLRUAN
OS Map (1:50,000) 200 or
OS Map (1:25,000) SX 05/15
Length: approximately five miles.

This is a circular walk, making use of two ferries over the River Fowey. It is also a walk of which we never tire because it gives us marvellous views at any time of year and a complete absence of traffic.

You can leave your car in the car-park beside the Bodinnick Ferry in Fowey, but before you cross to Bodinnick you may wish to stock up with provisions in the old town, or maybe call for a drink or a coffee at one of the riverside hotels

The car ferry between Fowey and Bodinnick. The Hall Walk starts by walking up the hill past the inn to a footpath towards Polruan.

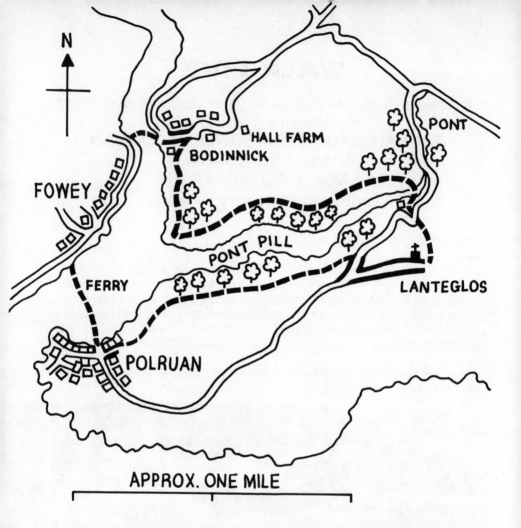

N

FOWEY

HALL FARM

BODINNICK

PONT

FERRY

PONT PILL

LANTEGLOS

POLRUAN

APPROX. ONE MILE

where you can sit and enjoy the view of vessels of all sizes passing by.

Cross the river by the ancient Bodinnick ferry which was certainly here (in a simpler form) in the fourteenth century and marked part of the route into Cornwall from Plymouth, using first the Cremyll ferry over the Tamar. On the opposite bank is the Old Ferry Inn, where lunchtime snacks are available.

Toiling up the steep hill, you will find a footpath marked on the right-hand side of the road: 'Hall Walk – Polruan – four miles'. This very pleasant and much-walked track leads south to Penleath Point, then east to the head of Pont Creek and back south-west to Polruan. The high walk affords wonderful views over Fowey (town and river) and leads through woods, fields and past ancient quays, mostly on land owned by the National Trust.

After only a short distance along the

The granite memorial to Sir Arthur Quiller-Couch with his beloved Fowey as a background. This view is from the path to Polruan, before reaching Pont.

Hall Walk we found a plaque beside a seat, stating: 'Hall Walk is written of by Carew in his Survey of Cornwall, 1602, as "a place of diversified pleasings." King Charles narrowly escaped death when a shot killed a poor fisherman who was standing at the place where the king had stood but a short while before.

A little further on, above Penleath Point at the confluence of the River Fowey and Pont Pill, you will find a large, roughly-hewn granite obelisk with the simple letter 'Q' chiselled into it, together with four coats of arms connected with the beloved town, county, college and family of Sir Arthur Quiller-Couch.

I always think how well sited is this memorial to the famous scholar and Cornishman who died in 1944, overlooking Fowey where he lived, the church and the great house called Place. It was here that he was once mayor and one of its few freemen.

The path now winds east alongside the creek of Pont Pill, through trees, eventually descending to a perfect picnic spot – a small quay with a lawn-like surface and a little footbridge. Like most other estuary creeks with deep water, there is a lime-burning kiln. Pasties, bacon sandwiches and hard-boiled eggs have been enjoyed by us here on several occasions.

The path now climbs quite steeply, crosses a minor road, and continues up a valley to the lovely Lanteglos-by-Fowey church with its surrounding farmyard. Its bench ends are worth seeing as they have Disney-like heads, others depicting local flowers, birds and trees. You may also get that 'Chamber of Horrors' feeling when you see the medieval alabaster carving of the martyrdom of St Lawrence being burnt alive on a grid, with an unpleasant chap wielding a bellows to keep the fire going. In a niche in the wall of the north aisle stands a figure of St Wyllow (sometimes spelt Wilow, Vylloe or Winwaloe) in whose name the church is dedicated. As you leave the south porch, notice the lovely old lichen-covered lantern cross standing outside.

We now follow a very narrow lane heading west until it joins a minor road. Turn right here for a few yards until you see the entrance to the walk on the left. The remainder of the walk along North Downs, on the south side of Pont Pill, is also truly delightful with beautiful views through the trees down to the water and across to Fowey. This section of the walk can be a little slippery underfoot after wet weather, so step carefully.

Eventually the path descends gently to old Polruan. It was more important than Fowey back in the eleventh century, but today its charm, for me, is the absence of traffic and noise. After exploring its narrow streets and attractive houses, make your way to the harbour where you can catch a ferry back across the water to Fowey. We usually stop for a jam and cream tea before making our way back along the main street to our car.

If you are not already familiar with this popular walk, do try it. It is at its best when the trees are in full leaf, but the views down over the busy river and quiet creek are almost as attractive when the trees are bare. And if you have a dog, take it along as it will enjoy plenty of freedom running about and foraging among the leaves.

Pont makes a perfect halfway point in the walk for a picnic.

WALK SIX

A walk of contrasts, from rocky coastline to quiet
wooded valley.
TREVALGA TO ST NECTAN'S GLEN
OS Maps (1:50,000) 190 & 200 or
OS Map (1:25,000) SX 08/18
Length: approximately four miles.

This beautiful walk along the high coast of North Cornwall and through a deep wooded valley falls annoyingly across two Ordnance Survey (1:50,000) maps. Fortunately, it can be followed in its entirety on the larger-scale (1:25,000) Camelford map in the excellent 'Pathfinder' series.

To start our walk we have to find our way to the little hamlet of Trevalga, midway between Tintagel and Boscastle, off the B3263 road. Here we find a few slate cottages with tilting roofs and a tiny church, dedicated to St Petroc. Its history goes back to Norman times and it is almost surrounded by a farmyard.

The size of the hamlet can be judged from the electoral roll that we saw pinned in the church porch, which num-

The interior of the tiny church at Trevalga.

View from the coastal path near Trevalga looking towards Boscastle.

bered the population at just 19. The interior of the weathered old church was largely restored in 1875, but a few bits of the original roof have survived.

Walk north, past the farm and along a lane past the entrance to a manor house, towards the sea, glittering in the distance. The track soon joins the coastal footpath where you turn left at a waymark.

The high cliffs here are a challenge to rock climbers as they include rocky needles and outcrops. We spotted a cairn of stones on one pinnacle that seemed to be 'unclimbable', and as you head west along the cliff top, you will notice a natural hole in one cliff, known as Ladies Window. It seems like a framed seascape of grandeur – especially on a day of wind and rough seas.

As you walk beside the cliff top walls with their distinctive herring-bone pattern, you may also notice hundreds of

Ladies Window – a natural hole in the rocks and the perfect place for a picnic using a nearby seat.

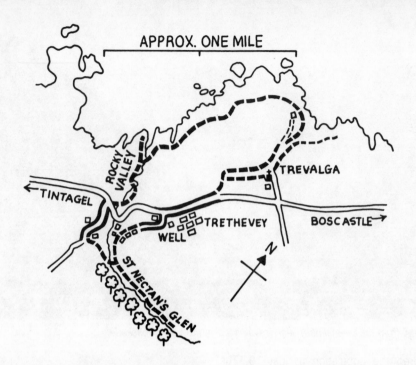

sea-birds wheeling over the sea and soaring up to their nests on the sheer rock face. This whole stretch of coast is famous for the variety of sea-birds it attracts, and it might be a good idea to carry a field guide to birds in your pocket.

The footpath curves south-west, past Saddle Rocks and a deep cleft in the cliff known as Trewethet Gut, until it eventually plunges down into Rocky Valley, with its stream cascading into the sea in such a way that it can only be appreciated as a waterfall from a boat.

Follow the stream inland through a steep-sided, well-wooded gorge until you reach the ruins of a mill. On the rocky wall here are two small carvings of mazes, possibly dating from the Bronze Age and preserved by the Department of the Environment.

You will shortly arrive at Trevillett Mill, built in 1475, where you can enjoy a rest and a cup of coffee in the delightful garden, and possibly meet the family goat. From here a steep road leads up to the busy B3263, and almost opposite – slightly to your left – is a minor road which straggles south for a quarter of a mile or so to Halgabron.

Shortly after passing some buildings on your left, a footpath sign directs you down across a sloping field to the dense woods of St Nectan's Glen. Continue through the trees until you descend to a bridge and cross the stream. The path on your left – leading back down the valley – is the one we will take on our return journey.

But first, walk east along and up the valley beside the stream. This deep, quiet, ferny valley, with green light filtering through the leaves above, is in

36

The beautiful path through the woods leading to the waterfall and St Nectan's Kieve.

great contrast to the high, breezy cliff top of the first stage of this walk.

After a short distance, the path begins to climb up the hillside to the little teahouse and a dramatic waterfall. The water was thundering down when we were there into a highly-polished bowl, giving rise to its name – St Nectan's Kieve (St Nectan's Bowl). It was once the home of a holy man of whom many legends abound and who was probably a sixth-century saint. The sun rarely reaches down into the hollow and it fosters a host of ferns of all varieties. We noticed the bright colouring of the stones in this stream – they appear as a surface element so we wondered if it passed through some strata of mineral on its way to the sea.

This whole valley is a place of peace, quiet and mystery which must have been loved by Thomas Hardy, who lived a mile or so away. It was the subject of his poem 'Under The Waterfall'.

I think it must have also been known to Sir Frances Drake as, in 1584, he was Member of Parliament for nearby Bossiney, one of the pre-1832 'rotten boroughs'.

Retracing your steps down the glen, and continuing to the right of the stream when you reach the wooden bridge, the path slowly climbs and becomes a road as it passes some houses. As it veers north-east, the road passes some very ancient buildings and leads you to another tiny church and, opposite, St Piran's Well.

Leaving the hamlet of Trethevey, follow the main road towards Boscastle for a short distance before taking a footpath across a field and a farm lane directly back to the farmyard beside Trevalga church.

There is something for everybody on this walk, and it is equally beautiful in spring, summer or autumn, when the leaves in St Nectan's Glen turn gold.

WALK SEVEN

A popular walk from one of Cornwall's most unspoilt villages, along spectacular coastline to an idyllic valley, returning by way of stiles and fields.
MOUSEHOLE TO LAMORNA
OS Map (1:50,000) 203 or OS Map (1:25,000) SW 32/42
Length: approximately five miles.

We begin this walk in Mousehole, a sheer delight of narrow, cobbled streets, alleys, cottages, working boats, nets and crab pots. There is even an Elizabethan manor house right in the centre of the village.

The village was raided and burnt by the Spaniards in 1595 and this was just one of the tragedies that it has suffered. Hanging over the harbourside is the famous Lobster Pot Hotel, where

Dylan Thomas spent his honeymoon with Caitlin, and facing out over the cluster of boats is the Ship Inn, renowned for its celebrations on Tom Bawcock's Eve – 23rd December – when Starry-Gazey Pie is eaten. Is it too much to hope that one day Mousehole will be traffic free?

The walk from Mousehole to Lamorna is a traditional outing for villagers on Good Friday. Earlier this cen-

The harbour at Mousehole, at low tide.

Mousehole from the harbour with unusual clock and war memorial.

tury walkers wore their best suits and dresses for the event and it was a far more sedate affair than of late.

We begin by turning away from the harbour and toiling up a metalled road, Raginnis Hill, passing the little Bird Hospital and Sanctuary founded by those wonderful selfless sisters called Yglesias and now run by the RSPCA. Near the top of the hill you will find the coastal footpath on your left-hand side. For two miles it follows the contours of the coastline with wonderful views down to the rocky coast and the sea. At one point the path passes through a copse of trees which we found most unusual and charming, and in summer and autumn the whole of this sloping coastal hillside is covered with high bracken.

On the way we passed the wreck of a modern trawler which ploughed into the rocks and made that its final resting place. At some points the path goes up and down quite steeply and my wife walked at a crouched angle reminding me of her fear of heights and consequent vertigo.

Eventually we were rewarded by the sight of Lamorna Cove with its little harbour, quay and quarry and its beautiful tree-lined valley and stream coming all the way down to the sea. It was not difficult to see why this place is so famous in the world of art and its associations with Lamorna Birch.

Walking up the valley, with the small river gushing between rocks to your right, you reach the diminutive village with its post office and inn, known as 'The Wink'. The right fork leads down to the river and over an ancient bridge to Kemyel Mill where corn was ground until the 1920s.

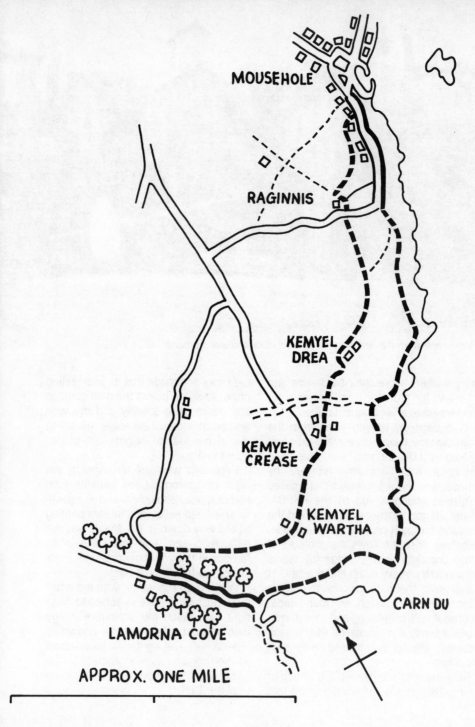

MOUSEHOLE

RAGINNIS

KEMYEL
DREA

KEMYEL
CREASE

KEMYEL
WARTHA

CARN DU

LAMORNA COVE

N

APPROX. ONE MILE

The small pier at Lamorna Cove – surely one of Cornwall's most beautiful places. A stream gushes down the valley to the sea.

Following the steep road beside the water wheel to a hairpin bend, you will see a stile and a footpath sign on the right, by a gate. The path climbs slowly along the valley side through bracken and gorse, with several old granite stiles. When you reach a dead tree, turn left and up over some rocks to the valley top and the farm of Kemyel Wartha. Follow the signs and walk left, between the buildings.

This footpath takes you all the way back to Mousehole by way of stiles, fields and farms, with wonderful views down over the coast and out to sea. As you approach the hamlet of Kemyel Crease, aim for the right side, crossing a stone stile, then pass between the buildings. The path now descends to a rather boggy area, then climbs again to Kemyel Drea. As you reach the hamlet, turn left along the road for a few yards, then follow the sign on the right, crossing some wooden stiles and passing between the buildings once again.

After an exhilarating walk across the high fields, you cross the road to the 'Raginnis Farm' sign, walk between the buildings then bear right through the hamlet with a charming thatched farmhouse on your left. From this point several paths lead back down to Mousehole. The casual tourist seldom climbs up through the village to the top of the hill, but on this walk we suddenly come across this point where we see the village displayed in front of us with Mount's Bay as a backdrop.

Incidentally, if you see scaffolding structures in the fields above the village

Return to Mousehole at the end of the walk – a view most tourists do not see!

and wonder about their purpose, they are the basis for some of Mousehole's charming Christmas illuminated set-pieces. The whole village seems to be lit by twinkling lights in December and the illuminations draw regular visitors from all over West Cornwall.

The walk I have described is just under five miles in length. For those interested in a slightly longer walk, there is a pleasant deviation at Lamorna by walking further up the valley and finding the footpath to one of Cornwall's most famous circles of stones – the Merry Maidens. There are 19 stones and the circle is 75 feet in diameter, with two larger stones, The Pipers, in nearby fields. They are connected by a legend with King Athelstan (AD 895-940), the founding of St Buryan and the last battle between the English and the Cornish in AD 935.

From the Merry Maidens, return to Lamorna by the same route and continue as for the shorter walk.

WALK EIGHT

Creeks, castles and clematis.
SALTASH TO ANTONY PASSAGE
OS Map (1:50,000) 201 or OS Map (1:25,000) SX45
Length: approximately two or four miles.

It was a fine day in early summer when we decided to find an interesting morning's walk before we visited Ince Castle in the afternoon.

We started our walk from the ancient fifteenth-century Church of St Stephens, the mother church of Saltash, which is on top of a hill with fine views across to Trematon Castle, the Lynher River, the famous Hamoaze and a more distant view of Mount Edgcumbe across the river. The church is nearly a mile west of Saltash and often missed by those hurrying to a crossing of the Tamar.

If you wish to reach the starting point by rail, take the train to Saltash station

The Church of St Stephens by Saltash. The churchyard contains many finely carved gravestones.

The ancient creekside village of Forder in the valley below Trematon Castle.

and walk to the main street, passing the old chapel of St Nicholas and St Faith and the seventeenth-century Guildhall. This adds another two miles to your walk, but the contrast between the sight of cars pouring over the road bridge into the tunnel, the bustling shopping streets, and the tranquillity and beauty of the rest of the walk is very striking. To reach the church, follow the main street west, bearing left along St Stephen's Road just before reaching the school. Continue along this road and you will soon see the church before you, with a fine view of Trematon Castle beyond.

The roof of the church was obviously restored in 1866 as that date is picked out in coloured slates. I am fascinated by ancient sundials and the latin legend on the one over the porch was difficult to decipher because of the weathering of the years. Finally it told us 'The sun rules me, the shadows you'. Perhaps my favourite one is at St Wenn, which warns you 'Ye Know Not When'.

We walked past the Cecil Arms and down a very steep hill to the pretty little creekside village of Forder. Take the lower of two metalled roads which winds along beside the creek under high oak and beech trees, loud with bird-song when we were there. Leaving behind the shadow of Trematon Castle and with the rotting hulks of old vessels stuck deep in the mud, we passed under the giant viaduct that carries the London-Penzance main line. How often I have looked down from the carriage at this quiet little creek. The whole of this walk was made even more delightful by the well-kept gardens on either side. For a clematis-lover, it was a sheer treat and I envied the fact that whatever the soil is here, clematis love it and thrive with a wealth of colour. Lilac, too,

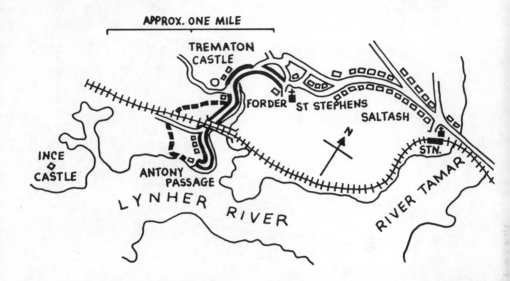

APPROX. ONE MILE

seems to prosper here and the scent was sometimes almost overpowering.

After passing beneath the arches of the viaduct, turn left at the next junction. Ahead we see a small cluster of buildings so familiar to all rail passengers as they peer down from their speeding 125. It is Antony Passage and most of the mill buildings alongside the creek are very old – one bears the date 1613. The views from the small harbour across the Lynher River are delightful, and we are now opposite Jupiter Point where the Royal Naval Sailing Club is so idyllically situated.

On the morning of our walk, the river was teeming with sailing dinghies with multicoloured sails, and all against the background of a wooded hillside with glimpses of Antony House between the trees.

On the inland side of the path are the obvious remains of an old railway line (marked on my map as a 'dismantled

An ancient doorway of a house in Forder (1613).

45

Striding across the creek is the main-line railway viaduct.

railway'). What intrigued us was that someone had made a long, shrub-lined lawn from the original track – one of Cornwall's most unusually-shaped gardens, I should think. This marked one of Isambard Kingdom Brunel's few mistakes in the planning of the railway route into Cornwall. He abandoned this route in the early stages, but the traces are still here.

The minor road gives way to a path which follows the side of the river, below some stone buildings, then up some steps and through trees until you reach a tunnel under the railway line. Upon emerging, a path leads northwest and up across fields to a high point from where you get a fine view up and down the river, with Ince Castle across a near-side creek.

I know of no building in Cornwall like it, with its tower at each corner. It was built by the Killigrew family and a legend says that one member of that family had a wife in each tower! Descending into a valley and crossing the minor road and railway line, the route now climbs up across another field, passing east of the sturdy walls of Trematon Castle before dropping to Forder once more. From here we retrace our steps up to the church. But remember you have to negotiate that steep hill, so first, take advantage of the seat thoughtfully provided by the creek at Forder.

The creekside part of this walk makes a good dry stroll at any time of year – cutting out the return across the fields – and in high summer the sights, sounds and flowery smells of this waterside walk are especially relaxing.

WALK NINE

A walk across some of Cornwall's most remote moorland.
ST BREWARD TO KING ARTHUR'S HALL
OS Maps (1:50,000) 200 & 201 or
OS Map (1:25,000) SX 07/17
Length: approximately eight miles.

This is a lonely moorland walk to what is, in my opinion, the remotest spot in Cornwall, on Bodmin Moor. I should perhaps add that the walk I suggest is 'one way', returning by the outward route, but the more able-bodied who wish to make a full day of it can lengthen the walk, returning by a different route.

We start from the village of St Breward, at 730 feet above sea level one of the highest in Cornwall, with all the houses built of granite from the nearby De Lank quarry.

The wonderfully solid church is dedicated to St Breward, Brueredus or Branwalader (the Raven Lord), who lived here in the sixth century. The original Norman walls of the chancel, the font and some of the pillars remain, but

Outside St Breward church in one of Cornwall's highest villages.

Alex Tor is just 1000 feet above sea level and the rock formations make a picnic comfortable whichever way the wind is blowing.

the wagon roof, tower and south porch date from the fifteenth century. The whole interior was restored by J.P. St Aubyn in 1864.

In the chancel we noticed a slate slab dedicated to John Adams, the local vicar who died in 1609, that illustrated for posterity the dress fashionable at the time of the Spanish Armada, with ruffs and outrageous hats. Over the porch a sundial dated 1792 is carved with the timely reminder: 'Seize the moments as they fly, know to live and learn to die'.

We also noticed a sign over the door of the Old Inn telling us that this is the highest licensed premises in Cornwall – a boast it could probably share with one or two other inns. It is a comfortable place and you may wish to take

advantage of the bar snacks before or, more likely, after your walk.

From the inn, walk south-east along the road and turn left at the first junction, heading east for a short distance before turning right at the 'No Through Road' sign to Casehill and The Candras. Follow this narrow road heading roughly north-east as it climbs slowly across boulder-strewn moorland, resembling a moon landscape. On reaching the top of the rise a marvellous panorama of distant moorland spreads out before you, with the jagged heights of Roughtor – seen 'end-on' from this position – and Brown Willy directly in front of you. A short deviation across to Alex Tor (just 1000 feet above sea level) for a picnic is worthwhile.

The narrow road descends to the

From Alex Tor distant views of Rough Tor, Brown Willy, Garra Tor, Hawks Tor and even Caradon Hill are visible.

farmsteads of Candra, Middle Candra and across a ford to Casehill. A board alongside the small stream is marked to a depth of six feet, and we found it difficult to imagine this same quiet valley after winter snow or rain with a deep, swirling torrent gushing through it.

The less energetic may wish to come this far by car. If so, remember not to block the road or anyone's gateway with your car. After crossing the ford, we struck out eastwards into the open moor, along the north side of a stone wall, to the archaeological treat of the day – the huge King Arthur's Hall. The excavation has been fenced and is quite unlike anything I have seen before. I find myself wondering what it looked like in its heyday.

The high walls of this large rectangular enclosure are lined with tall granite slabs, but the interior is now very boggy. Could it have been a meeting-hall, covered with a wooden roof? Or perhaps the setting for religious ceremonies? According to Craig Weatherhill in his useful book Cornovia (Alison Hodge, 1985) its date and purpose are still a mystery, but similar structures in Wales and Ireland are neolithic.

This entire walk is through sheep country, not to mention small herds of cattle, including a few long-horned highland cattle. So it is essential to close all gates firmly behind you and to make sure that, if you have brought your dog for some moorland exercise, it is kept under control on a lead at all times.

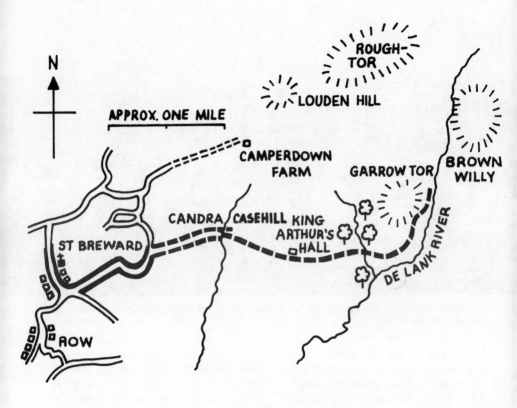

Walking east and slightly downhill we continued across the moor until we reached a small valley with a plantation running approximately north-south. After passing through a gate we came to a boulder-strewn stream of clear and, in places, very deep water. A short distance downstream is a bridge, an ideal spot for a rest. After passing through the plantation, struggling through the branches of fir trees, we emerged into dramatic empty moorland with the De Lank River on our right and the towering mass of Garrow Tor on our left.

We followed the faint outline of a track round the foot of Garrow Tor and past the little granite house of Garrow, where we were greeted by three delightful students holidaying there who offered us a cup of tea. Afterwards we worked out that they must have left their car at least one and a half miles away so their holiday luggage must have been kept to a minimum!

50

The footpath passes a granite farmhouse on the lower slopes of Garrow Tor, with Brown Willy in the distance.

Our path now led down to a ford across the small river and here we enjoyed a picnic, saw a heron and buzzards and swam in a deep pool further upstream. It was the middle of the tourist season, yet here we were enjoying real peace and solitude at the foot of Cornwall's highest point – Brown Willy (1377 feet).

From here we retraced our steps to St Breward, refreshed and happy. But if you feel energetic and allow yourself enough time, you may wish to climb to the summit of Brown Willy, descending the north-western side to cross the river again and continue to the top of Roughtor. The views from both these high points are magnificent and are described in Book One of this series.

Whichever route you take, perhaps I should add my usual warning that there is little if any shelter anywhere along the way, so check the weather forecast carefully before setting off onto the open moor.

Garrow Farm – is it the most remote on Bodmin Moor?

WALK TEN

Wide panoramas of the busy maritime life in Carrick
Roads form the background to this walk.
FLUSHING TO MYLOR CHURCHTOWN
OS Map (1:50,000) 204 or OS Map (1:25,000) SW 83
Length: approximately four miles.

As this walk begins and ends at the charming little port and fishing village of Flushing, you can either drive there directly or take the ferry across from Falmouth. If you decide on the latter, make sure of the time of the last return ferry before you set off.

We begin the walk by taking the road east to Trefusis Point, a route which we took on a previous walk from Penryn described in Book Two of this series. In fact, those keener walkers among my readers may wish to link the two walks together, setting off from Penryn and following the path round to Mylor before returning to Flushing.

Taking the high road out of Flushing, past delightful houses with turrets, towers and tall chimneys, we soon descend to the tiny, restored pier at Trefusis. Backtracking a little, we take the path which continues through the base of Kilnquay Wood before emerging onto an open field and following the

Flushing quay with evidence of its commercial fishing. Falmouth can be seen on the other side of the river.

Tranquillity at Flushing.

Looking across at busy Falmouth.

Walking from Trefusis Point, this is the first view one has of Mylor dockyard – it is crowded with boats throughout the year.

coast to Trefusis Point itself. From here you look out across the river to Falmouth and the quays of the docks, which reach almost half way across the river, directly towards you.

Following the path north-east, with a hillside of trees and gorse on your left, the view out onto Carrick Roads is superb. In the centre is the dreaded Black Rock and beyond are St Just Pool, St Anthony lighthouse and St Mawes. As you near Penarrow Point, you can look across the waterway to Messack Point, the limit of Truro's authority as a port. Most of this stretch of path is cut by ridges to allow drainage, and while they are cut a little short for my step, at least they keep the path dry after rainy weather.

Throughout the length of this walk there is constant activity on the water to your right: ferries, tugs, canoes, speedboats, wind-surfers, fishing boats, deep-sea trawlers, ocean-going yachts and harbour-bound dinghies. Shortly after rounding Penarrow Point you may catch a glimpse of a granite pillar down on the beach. This marks the official boundary between Falmouth and Truro.

Soon you will reach Mylor Dockyard, which is said to be the smallest in the country. It is a favourite mecca for yachtsmen from France as well as locals, and has a busy marina and service station as well as an excellent restaurant. In the 1850s it was the shore port of HMS Ganges and still has

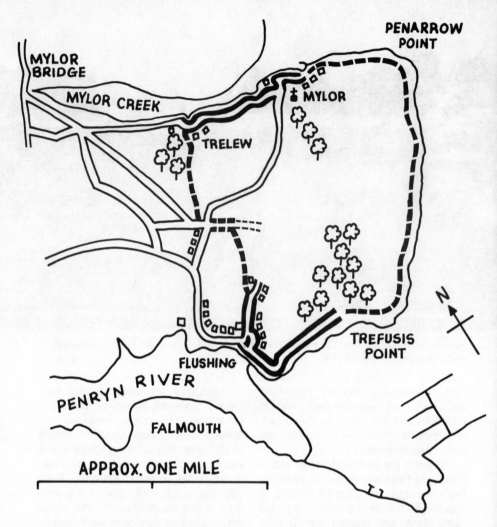

MYLOR BRIDGE

MYLOR CREEK

TRELEW

MYLOR

PENARROW POINT

TREFUSIS POINT

FLUSHING

PENRYN RIVER

FALMOUTH

N

APPROX. ONE MILE

the original Captain's House, used while the training ship was afloat in Carrick Roads. The parish church of Mylor is well worth visiting and we were there during a flower festival when it looked particularly beautiful. Cornwall's tallest granite cross (17 feet above the ground, with several feet below) stands just outside the lovely

south porch with its elaborately carved arch. Inside is an Elizabethan pulpit and memorials to the Trefusis, Bonython and Lemon families. The tower, with its Norman door, has a small single turret, and the detached bell tower to the south-west of the church contains three bells.

The graveyard rewarded us with

Mylor church with Carrick Roads beyond. The tallest celtic cross stands before the south porch. A favourite place for those who research epitaphs.

many epitaphs, some tragic and others very descriptive. Here are the mass graves of 136 men drowned when the Queen Transport was wrecked off Trefusis Point in 1814, and those drowned when the pleasure boat Darlwyn foundered near the Dodman Head in 1966. Cornwall's best-known epitaph records the death, aged 43, of Joseph Crapp who fell from the topmost mast of a schooner in Falmouth in 1770.

Alass Frend Joseph,
His end was all most sudden,
As though a mandate came
Express from Heaven –
His foot, it slip, and he did fall.
Help help he cries, and that was all.

Another epitaph records the death of an innocent man rowing across from St Just to Mylor who was 'shot in excess of zeal by an Excise man'.

Leaving by the lychgate at the top of the churchyard, follow an unmade-up track almost opposite, beside a house named Angarrack. This is the little-used Church Road which winds behind some attractively sited houses, all with gardens flowing down to private creekside moorings, towards Mylor Bridge.

You may wish to extend this walk by continuing along the path to Mylor Bridge, returning to Flushing along the road, or even further by heading north from Mylor Bridge to the next creek at Restronguet, with its delightful Pandora Inn.

However, to continue our shorter walk, you follow the path as far as the valley of Trelew where a path cuts off to the left to Trelew farm. After passing through a gate, and just before a second gate, a small track on the left leads down and round the farm. Following the signs, the track burrows up the hillside under a canopy of branches. After ducking under several arches formed by fallen trees, the path emerges into a field and eventually onto a road.

Turn left and at a crossroads keep straight ahead, past a sign saying 'Private Road – Public footpath only'. Just before reaching a house, a gateway on the right leads to a footpath which descends across a large field.

The panorama across the water to Falmouth, with its windmill on the horizon, is magnificent. The path soon descends to a housing estate and into the valley which winds up behind Flushing. The quiet streets of colour-washed houses in this unspoilt little town form a pleasant end to this easy and varied walk.

WALK ELEVEN

Two short woodland walks in a little-known valley.
HERODSFOOT AND ALONG THE WEST LOOE RIVER
OS Map (1:50,000) 201
Length: approximately two and three miles.

These two short walks, both through Forestry Commission woodland, take us through a former deer park and alongside the West Looe River. The short drive between the two walks passes through the charming village of Herodsfoot. As these walks cover four of the large-scale 1:25,000 Ordnance Survey maps, you are probably safer to stick solely with the good old 1:50,000 pink-covered map.

To find the starting point in the picnic area of Deerpark Wood, we left the A390 at Middle Taphouse – a few miles west of Liskeard – and headed south along the B3359 towards Pelynt and Looe.

After about three miles, we took the lane leading east towards Herodsfoot. After less than a mile we found the entrance to Deerpark Wood on our right and a sign leading to the Forest Trail. Parking the car we set off on a circular walk. We were shut off from the rest of the world the whole morning in dense woodland with acres of bluebells, prim-

A clearing in Deerpark Wood, with tables kindly provided for the inevitable picnic.

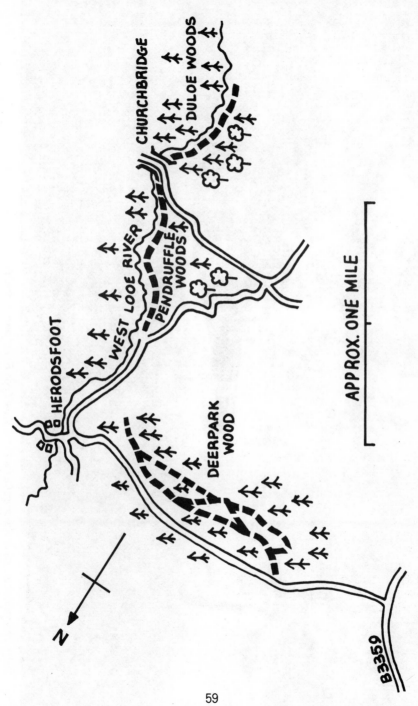

HERODSFOOT

WEST LOOE RIVER

PENDRUFFLE WOODS

CHURCHBRIDGE

DULOE WOODS

DEERPARK WOOD

APPROX. ONE MILE

N

B3359

The charming little village of Herodsfoot with the West Looe River flowing through it.

Church Bridge near Pendruffle wood, between Herodsfoot and Looe.

roses and other wild flowers along paths that took us downhill, nearly to the West Looe River – an ugly 'Private' notice barred our exit to it – and then along the other side of the valley back up to our car.

Near the car-park are benches and tables tucked away in the woods and the only other human being of the morning was sitting beside his car reading the Financial Times and with a portable colour television in use! After sandwiches and coffee among the bluebells we turned right, downhill, with forest on either side, to Herodsfoot.

At the foot of the hill we turned right and drove south, but not before stopping off to enjoy this lovely village, set in a deep, wooded valley and with a little church perched on the hillside above. There are some charming cottages and a small bridge over the river that winds through the village.

The road south from Herodsfoot follows the valley for a while, then, just before it veers to the right, uphill, we found another Forestry Commission car-park on the left, at the entrance to Pendruffle Woods. We followed the public bridle path from here all the way alongside the river bank to Churchbridge. We saw many inviting glades and grassy banks for picnic sites to be noted for future occasions.

Always in our ears was the sound of the fast-running river meandering down the valley, and Tessa, our dachshund, was in her element and enjoyed paddling in the shallows. The sound of birdsong was also particularly loud in this deep valley.

After a brief spell of metalled lane at Churchbridge, we continued downstream on the same side of the river through Duloe Woods, until it was time to retrace our steps. We could have made a circular walk by climbing west out of the valley at Churchbridge and returned to our car by little lanes, passing the entrance to Pendruffle farm. But we were so enchanted by the bridlepath that we decided we would return the same way. Such a level path is unusual for us and quite a treat!

This is a little-known Cornish valley and nearby is the charming village of Lanreath with its museum of antique agricultural implements, cider press and farmhouse. It surprises me that even tractors can be antique – or is the word vintage? Also nearby is the village of St Keyne with its holy well half a mile east of the village. This is a 'must' if you are newly married as the legend suggests that whichever of the married couple drinks its water first will wear the matrimonial trousers. We decided that we could not have found a more peaceful and beautiful walk at bluebell time and that a good long-distance walk would be to follow the river right down to the sea and wish it farewell, standing at the end of the Banjo Pier at Looe!

WALK TWELVE

By foot to a war memorial fishing village.
TO PENBERTH COVE AND ST LOY
OS Map (1:50,000) 203 or OS Map (1:25,000) SW 32/42
Length: approximately five miles.

To find the starting point of this walk, leave Newlyn on the B3315, heading towards Treen and Porthcurno. A couple of miles after passing the Merry Maidens stone circle, you will see a notice and entrance to Treverven campsite on your left, with a small wooded valley beyond. If you have travelled by car, try to leave your car somewhere near this point.

The walk proper begins by following a track to the left, just before the wood, across a cattle grid and uphill through Burnewhall farm. Note the date 1849 on the wall. Follow the farm lane going south, with distant views of the sea and the Logan Rock, with Treen just inland south-westwards. The 'hedges' are composed of irregular blocks of granite, and when we last walked this way there was a profusion of wild flowers, particularly campions, and skylarks were singing high above us.

The lane becomes a path and eventually swings west across fields before joining the coastal footpath, which descends slowly to Penberth.

This unspoilt and traffic-free, simple,

Penberth Cove – a living memorial to those who died in the Second World War. A view from the path leading up to Cribba Head and the Logan Rock.

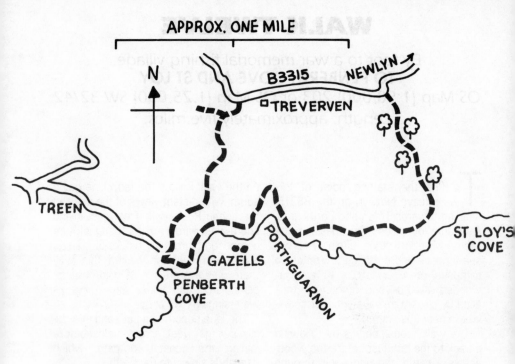

N

B3315

NEWLYN

TREVERVEN

TREEN

GAZELLS

PORTHGUARNON

PENBERTH
COVE

ST LOY'S
COVE

fishing hamlet is, in my opinion, Cornwall's most beautiful memorial to those who died in the Second World War. It was to their memory that it was transferred in 1957 to the National Trust through the National Heritage Fund.

We loved the granite footbridge over the stream just above the slipway, and Tessa enjoyed walking in the shallow water. We watched a fishing boat, The Grey Seal, approaching while we stood in the sea cooling our feet. One of the crew came ashore and, in a few minutes, a little engine came to life near the top of the slipway and a steel rope was attached and the boat and its catch went up the steep slope. There is also a huge wooden winding gear for hauling boats up the slipway.

This is a wonderfully temperate area and, in days gone by, the local fishermen all had allotments or fields where they grew early flowers and potatoes for sale as far away as London and the Midlands. You may wish to walk up the valley a short way and admire the fine old thatched cottages before retracing your steps up the cliffside along the coastal path.

Follow the path eastwards, overlooking rocks called the Gazells. Nine miles away to the south-west is the Wolf Rock lighthouse. The path now curves inland and a precipitous path takes you down to the stream flowing into the sea at Porthguarnon, where Tessa just lay down and let the stream tumble over her. We envied a lovely couple who had scrambled out onto the giant

A little stream rushes down the valley through Penberth with its thatched cottages and absence of cars.

Fishing boats are hauled up the granite slipway by a stationary engine.

On the path between Penberth and St Loy.

blocks of granite and were swimming in deep, clear, blue, open water by just stepping off their picnic spot.

Just afterwards we climbed, with frequent rests (to admire the view!) the steepest bit of the coastal path that we have ever tackled. But eventually we triumphed and we had our picnic on Merthen Point. From here we could see Boscawen Point in the foreground, with Tater-du lighthouse visible beyond it. Beyond that we could make out Lizard Point, the sands between Porthleven and Gunwalloe Cove and the giant satellite-tracking discs on Goonhilly Downs.

The coast path continues eastwards until it descends to an abrupt and startling change of environment at St Loy. The path now leads north-westerly inland, following a stream, until it reaches the B3315 near Treverven farm. This path is rather overgrown and we had to hack our way through bracken, stinging nettles and thorns with our walking sticks, but it is a beautiful path with the noise of the stream ever in our ears as we walked. I am six feet tall but the bracken was at times above my head, and my bare shoulders were stung by nettles!

Walking three quarters of a mile westwards along the B3315 finds us back at our starting point after a walk of peace and calm and contrast. Even with a strong wind blowing, you can enjoy some of the delights of this walk by driving down to Penberth Cove and walking the stretch of coastal footpath, and you may wish to add to your enjoyment of the day by calling in at the tidy little village of Treen, and walking across fields to see the Logan Rock and the amazing cliff castle of Treryn Dinas.

WALK THIRTEEN

A countryside walk beside the River Fal.
TREGONY TO GOLDEN MILL AND CREED CHURCH
OS Map (1:50,000) 204 or
OS Map (1:25,000) SW 94/SX 04
Length: approximately five miles.

Just beside the bridge over the River Fal below Tregony on the A3078, we found a perfect parking space to leave the car for the start of this walk.

Ships carrying wine, general merchandise and limestone from Brittany once came right up to this bridge and were tied up to an iron ring fixed to a rock in the river. It was recorded as being there in 1584 and 1733, but we saw no sign of it on our walk, so presumably it must now lie well below the mud and china-clay silt.

Climbing over a granite stile right on the bridge itself, we were immediately in water meadows walking northwards upstream, along the east bank of the river. There was complete peace and tranquillity, and not a soul did we see for the next hour at least. But we did see a heron slowly flapping away from its fishing spot a few yards ahead, and every possible variety of wild flower to be found in the water meadows.

We did this walk early one morning after recent rainfall, and parts of the path were quite muddy – so be pre-

The path follows the River Fal upstream from Tregony Bridge through water meadows.

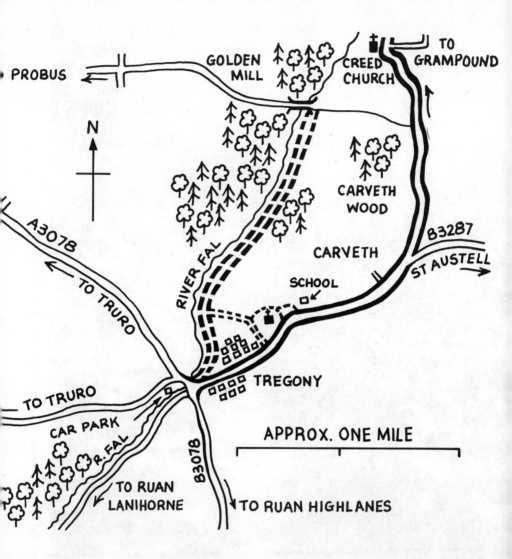

PROBUS

GOLDEN MILL

CREED CHURCH

TO GRAMPOUND

N

CARVETH WOOD

A3078

B3287

ST AUSTELL

RIVER FAL

TO TRURO

CARVETH

SCHOOL

TO TRURO

CAR PARK

R. FAL

TREGONY

APPROX. ONE MILE

B3078

TO RUAN LANIHORNE

TO RUAN HIGHLANES

pared! Tessa, our dog, was lagged with mud but very happy, and she was able to clean herself in the shallows of the river, sending trout darting upstream.

After about three quarters of a mile the path took us through a wood and we had to beat our way with sticks through the brambles. However, I gather from a more recent walker that someone has kindly cut all these back and cleared a well-defined path. Thank you. The rest of the path to Golden Mill lay beside the river to the accompanying sounds of skylarks and rooks (and one low-flying helicopter). A pair of buzzards wheeled and glided above – they

The path (still beside the River Fal) nears the idyllically situated Golden Mill amongst the woods.

Golden Mill.

love this sort of country.

Passing alongside a field of tall 'corn-on-the-cob', we reached the first bridge and the idyllic setting of Golden Mill. Whilst enjoying the atmosphere of solitude, we remembered the tragic happenings at nearby Golden Manor in 1577 when Saint Cuthbert Mayne, a Roman Catholic priest being hidden by Francis Tregian and his family, was captured and martyred at Launceston Castle. It is said that his tortured body was hung from the centre of the bridge at Wadebridge, but it seems unlikely to me. Francis Tregian was also imprisoned and stripped of his wealth and died in Lisbon in 1604. Turning right (east) we walked uphill by way of a gated road with increasingly wonderful

views as we got to the top. The pinnacle of the tower of Creed Church, half a mile to the north, St Stephen on the horizon and the woods of Trewithen and Trenowth were much in evidence. When we joined the metalled minor road we did a half-mile 'deviation' to visit Creed Church, and this proved very worthwhile.

Perhaps the most unusual items were two photographs of William Gregor, one of Creed's vicars (the first recorded was 1260!) who discovered the metal titanium near Manaccan, and another of a bowl made of the metal. These contrasted with the 700-year-old font nearby. From a seat in the churchyard we looked down to the Fal running just a field away as it must have been

The pleasantly preserved ancient church of Creed.

when the church was originally built and then rebuilt in 1734.

We returned to Tregony along country lanes and finally the busy B3287 with its fine view across to Cornwall's highest church tower at Probus. Tregony explored on foot is a real treat with lovely little alleys with cobbled surfaces, an inn with attractive pillars at its entrance and the peace of fourteenth-century St Cuby church with its wall-to-wall carpeting, sundial reminding you to 'Mind Your Time', twelfth-century font, wagon roof and pulpit partially made of old benchends.

The late, much-loved retired surgeon, Mr K.O. Parsons of Tregony, has recorded the story of Tregony's distinctive clock tower with two dates on it – 1833 and 1863. The first clock was a memorial to Richard Gurney, rector and magistrate, and had a single hand. It was bought by a Mr Dunstan in 1861 at an auction of Corporation property, and he proposed sending it to Australia. When he heard of this, the clock 'winder', a Mr Bawden, removed the clock and hid it. Finally Mr Dunstan accepted £12 compensation for not removing it, and the clock mysteriously reappeared. In 1863 the clock tower was restored and in 1928 the original clock was replaced by a 'modern' two-handed striking clock.

Finally we walked down to the bridge and put Tessa in the car and gave her a drink. It was lunchtime and we were made very welcome at the Kea House restaurant where we had a superb meal of fresh salmon and vegetables from their own garden.

This is a four-mile walk, but it stretches to five miles if you include the detour to Creed Church.

The Georgian Gothic clock tower in the main street of historic Tregony.

WALK FOURTEEN

An unusual waterside and woodland walk.
TO LOE POOL AND THE SEA
OS Map (1:50,000) 203 or OS Map (1:25,000) SW 52/62
Length: approximately four miles.

During my lifetime I have made many visits to Loe Pool, mainly by walking above the high-tide mark from Porthleven or by making the long five to six-mile walk around the pool from near Helston. But this account suggests quite a short walk that can be accomplished when you have less time or inclination for the full treatment.

The friendly owners of the Nansloe Manor Hotel told us of a lane that enables cars to travel to a car-park quite close to Carminowe Creek – the east-facing arm of Loe Pool. We found the lane, marked 'No Through Road' and right beside Helston hospital, which is near the roundabout where the A3083 meets the A394 near RNAS Culdrose.

The path from Degibna Chapel leads gently down to Carminowe Creek, Loe Bar and the sea.

The bar of sand between the sea and Loe Bar is an ideal picnic spot.

We followed it until we reached the little Methodist chapel at Degibna, opposite which is a large National Trust car-park.

We started our walk by continuing south-west along a lane with a signpost directing us to Loe Pool. This path afforded us increasingly wonderful views of the famous Loe Bar with the sea beyond. The path descends, past the keeper's house and a delightful picnic area, to the edge of the water. Here you turn left to walk around Carminowe Creek, passing a farmyard and a cottage – surely one of the National Trust's most remote and tranquil possessions.

At the eastern tip of the creek, a small bridge carries you over the stream and you continue along the opposite bank to the Loe Bar itself. Along this reed-fringed stretch we saw two herons and countless sea and wading birds.

Eventually you will reach the high shingle bank beyond which lies the sea. It is nearly always turbulent here and the surf looks, and indeed is, formidable and dangerous. A sign warns: 'Danger Beware – strong currents and freak waves. Swimming is inadvisable.' They might have added that even paddling is equally hazardous. The power of the waves, even on a moderately breezy day, is awesome.

It was here in 1807 that the frigate HMS Anson was wrecked. The great loss of life led to Henry Trengrouse perfecting the rocket life-saving apparatus that has been in use up until a year or

The sea is dangerous for swimming at all times at Loe Bar.

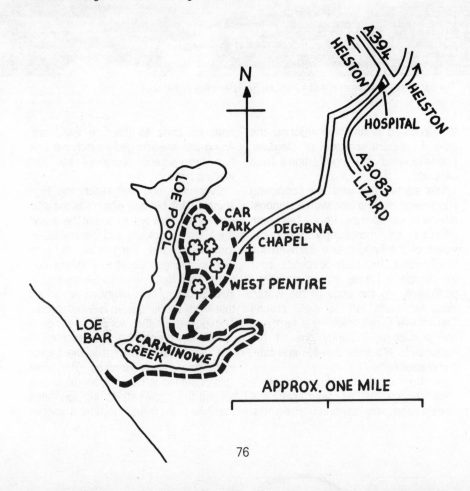

Just before the steep uphill climb back to Degibna is a good spot to stop to admire the view across *Loe Pool* to *Penrose*.

two ago when the decision was taken to dispense with it in favour of helicopter rescue.

Loe Pool is fed by the River Cober, and following excessive rainfall, the Pool sometimes overflows, covering many of the surrounding paths, especially in the Carminowe Creek area. In medieval times, records tell us that the Bar was cut to drain the Pool and it was said that the sea was so stained that it was detected as far away as Scilly. I would doubt it! Yet another legend says that a hand rising from the waters received the sword Excalibur, but that is said of many Cornish lakes, such as Dozmary Pool on Bodmin Moor.

We completed our walk by retracing our steps until, shortly after passing the cottage and farmhouse, a stile on the left allowed us to cross into a field and follow the path beside the lake. This path climbs through woodland of pine, oak and beech before descending to the lakeside again.

Shortly after crossing a stile into a plantation of young trees, a path on the right takes you up through a farmyard and onto a ridged, concreted lane which climbs steeply back to the carpark at Degibna. This path is so steep that you will almost certainly be glad of the excuse to pause for breath and look across the Pool to the mansion and gardens of the Penrose estate. In the 1740s a bitter dispute broke out between the Penrose family and the lord of the manor of Methleigh over who had the right of wreck between Porthleven and Loe Bar, and a lawsuit followed.

At whatever time of year you walk this route, it is difficult to find, in the space of one short walk, such a spectrum of flora and fauna.

WESTCOUNTRY BOOKS

Publishers of Great Walking Books

Cornwall Books ● Devon Books ● Exmoor Books ● Dorset Books

WALKING CORNWALL SERIES
Donald Vage

A tried and trusted series of three books covering walks throughout
the Duchy from one of the county's favourite authors.

Cornwall Books, £4.95 each

THE TARKA TRAIL

Based on Henry Williamson's famous *Tarka the Otter* story, the Tarka
Trail is one of Britain's newest long-distance footpaths. This official guide
covers the complete 180-mile circuit with short walks also included. Many
detailed maps and photos.

Devon Books, only £3.95

SECRETS OF THE MOOR
Chapman, Parker and Priestley

A walker's guide to the Exmoor landscape. A best-selling work published
in association with the successful Channel 4 television series.

Exmoor Books, £4.95 each

All these and many other walking guides
are available from:

**Westcountry Books
1 Chinon Court
Lower Moor Way
Tiverton, Devon EX16 1SS
Tel: 0884 243242
Fax: 0884 243325**

Send for a complete catalogue of our titles.